HANDLING
HUMANITY

POCKET EDITION

Published from
Mardukite Borsippa HQ, San Luis Valley, Colorado
Mardukite Academy & Systemology Society
for spiritual or educational purposes only

HANDLING HUMANITY

Systemology
Professional Course
Booklet #4

Developed by Joshua Free
for the Systemology Society

© 2023, JOSHUA FREE

ISBN : 978-1-961509-28-3

Pocket Paperback Edition — *November 2023*

mardukite.com

Learn How To Let Your Spirit Fly...

Then Chart Your Flight For Ascension!

Unlock your ultimate spiritual potential by removing barriers to your true native state.

Learn how to easily attain Self-actualization and help to actualize others along the way.

A greater appreciation and understanding of *Spiritual Life* and *Existence* awaits you. Expand your reach to achieve your dreams.

Each 'Professional Course' lesson-booklet offers simple exercises and techniques that directly apply the philosophy of Systemology, assisting to increase your true knowingness, improve your capabilities in this life, and even decide what you will do in your next.

At the Mardukite Academy of Systemology, the 'Professional Course' lessons in this series are presented to Seeker's that have completed the 'Basic Course', previously released as six lesson-booklets, or the six-in-one single volume edition "Fundamentals of Systemology."

This all new presentation of the Systemology 'Pathway-to-Ascension' takes Seekers and continuing students from "Zero" to "Infinity" at lightning-fast speeds!

Discover Who You Really Are...

Because You Were Never Human

TABLET OF CONTENTS

PROFESSIONAL
COURSE
INTRODUCTION

WELCOME, SEEKER!
LET'S CHART YOUR JOURNEY
ON THE PATHWAY

Systemology is a "holistic" approach to understanding the human experience. It is not actually a singular "subject" in itself, but rather, a new way in which to view the many subjects of *Life* and all *Existence*.

This is a professional course in *Systemology*—specifically, how to *apply* the spiritual philosophy of *Mardukite Systemology* as a personal *"Pathway" to Ascension.* Our *Systemology* is a new approach to *"Self-Actualization."* It is completely relevant for the modern age and the future; and quite different from any previous similar attempts, or other traditions, you might find. What's more: it is applicable to anyone with any background.

This *"Professional Course"* series of lessons (booklets) immediately follows the material given in the *"Basic Course"* series—available as six separate pocket-sized booklets, or in a single hardcover volume titled: *"Fundamentals of Systemology: A New Thought For The 21st Century."*

This is a *new* presentation of *Systemology*, emphasizing the application of our philosophy for those *Seekers* that are *"Flying-Solo"*—or else working through their studies and exercises as solitary practitioners. This is a new innovation for *Systemology*. Aside from the book *"Crystal Clear,"* all of our former advanced courses have placed a focus on *"Traditional Piloting"*—where experienced practitioners assist *Seekers* in *"processing."*

To receive the greatest benefit from this study: it is expected that a *Seeker* will already be familiar with the fundamental concepts and terminology (previously relayed in the *Basic Course*) before using lessons from the *Professional Course*. This will allow us to cover the extensive territory of the *Pathway* much more quickly. However, for reference, a basic *"glossary"* of vocabulary used in this lesson is provided in the *"appendix."*

A NEW VIEW OF THE HUMAN SPIRIT

Systemology is not a religion and does not require any type of *faith*. It is, however, built upon a "spiritual" premise—and as such is an "applied spiritual philosophy." It is based on ancient teachings that we are *Spiritual Beings* essentially "wearing" bodies like clothes—or using them as "vehicles." Yet our true native nature is not *physical*, but beyond this existence; and we can certainly operate a "body" from *outside* of it.

We are **all** *Spiritual Beings*—each of us a *unit* of *Spiritual Awareness*—that have experienced a very long *Spiritual Timeline* of existence. Although we might be particularly attached to the familiar "physical shells" associated with *this* lifetime, our true *"Spiritual Lifetime"* is seemingly *eternal*. We have been many things before *Human*, and we go onward as a *Spiritual Being* after our *"genetic vehicle"* of *this* incarnation perishes.

While a "spiritual" view of the *Human Condition* may not seem unique to our philosophy, just how often is the concept treated *systematically*? For that matter: just how many people, supposedly raised to this or that religion, or professing to believe one thing or another, actually live their lives as though they are *Spirits*?

As *Spiritual Beings* of immortal existence and infinite potential, we are not simply the *"creations"* of an even greater *Being-*

ness; we are, in fact, an integral part of that *"creative force"* which permeates all existence.

Our basic nature is to be a *"creative being"*—our highest goals are *"to create."* And as such a being—which we refer to as an *Alpha-Spirit* in *Systemology*—we have run into some difficulties along the course of our *Spiritual Timeline* and found ourselves trapped within material *Universes* of our own collaborative *creation*.

Since we did not start out our existence in a trapped condition, it is correct to say that we have *"fallen"* from our native *"godlike"* states. It did not happen all at one, but progressively and systematically. We know our "troubles" have resulted from accumulated "barriers" and "blockages"—or *fragmentation*—during our vast experiences as *Spiritual Beings*. They are not because we lack something; but because of what's been added.

In *Systemology*, we systematically examine those routes by which we must have descended to reach our present condition, then reverse the direction of travel and chart a personal *"Pathway to Ascension."* Of course, the exact "details" of the *Spiritual Timeline* will be different for each individual *Seeker*. However, we have been able to systematically chart our *Pathway* based on common patterns of *Human fragmentation*.

In the most basic terms: the *fragmentation* that defines our "downward spiral" consists of decisions or considerations where we deny our true nature. This includes those decisions to *"withdraw"* rather than *"reach"*; where we choose to *not-know* rather than *know*; to *not-communicate* rather than *communicate*; and ultimately, to take *no-responsibility* for being a *creative-cause*, and therefore succumb to being an *effect*.

But there is *hope!* And much more importantly: there is an effectively workable *way out* of the mazes and traps of our existence. If you are reading this now, you have already begun to gather your tools and build up the *"horsepower"* necessary to break the gravity holding your *Spiritual Beingness* to the *Human Condition.*

STUDYING THE PROFESSIONAL COURSE

Most *Seekers* study and practice *Systemology* at-a-distance and independent of the "Mardukite Academy" or any "Master-level" mentors trained therein. This means that the *books* (and to a lesser degree, the *internet*) are the only means of direct contact a *Seeker* maintains with the "Systemology Society" during their studies. A continuing *Seeker* from the *"Basic Course"* will be familiar with the style of study found in *this* course.

Misunderstood words are the most common reason an individual abandons studying a subject. When a misunderstanding occurs, *Awareness* declines. These misunderstandings start to "stack up" after the first occurrence, and as a result, the level of interest and attention will also decline. This is how a "confusion" develops; and the individual will get "bored" with the subject, feel tired, and unable to concentrate.

One solution is to return to the part of the material that was still interesting and enjoyable to read. When scanning around that area of text, there is likely to be a new word (or new specific use of a familiar word) that is unclear, but was passed by unnoticed. All *Systemology* books include their own *glossary*. Using this *glossary* and a high-quality dictionary will help resolve this misunderstanding once it is located.

An effective education of any subject is taught on a *gradient*. This is what is intended by presenting the study of something as *"grades."* Rather than treating a subject as one total mass, true learning is achieved by increasing one's understanding with a *gradual* increase upward. The *ascent* to a mountaintop is not successfully achieved in one leap, but by targeting and reaching specific checkpoints along the way.

This *Professional Course* consists of a series of lessons (booklets) that gradually increase a *Seeker's* ability to understand and apply the practices and techniques of *Systemology* as a complete *"Pathway to Ascension."* It is an appropriate study for continuing *Seekers* (from the *Basic Course*), but also "advanced" *Systemologists*.

Each lesson (booklet) of the *Professional Course* applies *Systemology* to a particular subject (or focus). It is best if the entire course can be studied and applied in sequential order. These lessons also employ a style of practice or technique called *"Systematic Processing."* An introduction to applying this methodology is provided in the final lesson (booklet) of the *Basic Course*—or in the *"Fundamentals of Systemology"* volume.

To study the *Professional Course* just like a student at the Academy: a *Seeker* reads through all instructional material and applies each exercise (or *"process"*) presented in the text to the extent they comfortably can, before continuing on to the next lesson (booklet).

When first starting on the *Pathway* as a *Solo* practitioner, without the aid of an experienced *Pilot*, a *Seeker* shouldn't "push too hard" or allow themselves to get too "stuck" on any one area (lesson) or *process*. It is not expected that any one area will be completely handled when first introduced. For optimum results, it is expected that a serious *Seeker* will make more than one "pass" through the entire *Professional Course.*

The *Professional Course* is not altogether different from other forms of practical or technical education: where the instruction and exercises are delivered to a completion, and then a student further increases their abilities, strength and skill-level by applying additional practice throughout their life. Therefore, a student should not concern themselves with perfectly mastering each step (or lesson) before progressing forward.

Additional passes through the material are likely to result in different *"realizations"* (an increased *level of understanding*) than a previous time. New "layers" of *Knowingness* may now be accessible during a *process* that may not have been before. It is important to avoid invalidating the progress you've made just because one area is not completely handled right away, or if a certain *process* seems too difficult on the first pass.

CHARTING A COURSE ON THE PATHWAY

Although we can communicate a systematic structure to *fragmentation,* the personal journey experienced along the *Pathway* will be different for each *Seeker.* For example, certain areas will seem more *"turbulent"* or difficult for one *Seeker* than another. We tend to say that these areas have more *"charge"* on them—or that they are more *"heavily charged."* It is best to handle such areas when you are already feeling "good" and not in a situation (or condition) where that specific area is consistently being *"triggered"* or *"restimulated."*

As an applied philosophy, *Systemology* "theory" can be easily utilized in the "laboratory" of the "world-at-large" in everyday life. This is implied within the basic instruction of each lesson. Unlike other "sciences" that conduct experiments by making a change to some "objective variable" *out there* and waiting to see an effect, our focus is the individual (or *Observer*) themselves, and how *they* affect the "*Reality*" perceived.

In addition to applying *Systemology* "New Thought" to everyday life, our philosophy is applied by using specific exercises and systematic techniques. These "*processes*" provide the most stable personal gain (and *realizations*) for each area; but only when actually applied with a *Seeker's* full "*presence*" and *Awareness*.

This *Professional Course* is designed so that it may be easily read and studied with little concern for what "dangers" these teachings—or *processing*—might unleash. However, there are still some guidelines that pertain to the "best-uses" of these course lessons, particularly if a *Seeker* intends for stable development.

Skipping over too much material/*processing* in early lessons may make attempts to understand (or apply) later lessons more difficult. However, once the complete *Professional Course* is worked through at least once in its entirety, specific areas can then be later returned to and treated with a greater sense of *Awareness* and *"presence"* than before. Of course, in *"Traditional Piloting,"* the rate of processing is monitored by an experienced practitioner; but in *"Solo-Processing,"* a *Seeker* must regulate their own progress on the *Pathway*.

Applying a systematic technique is called *"running a process."* The *processes* are designed with very simple instructions or *"command-lines."* To *run* a *processing command-line*, a *Seeker* may be assisted by the communication of that *line* from a *"Co-Pilot"* (as in *"Traditional Piloting"*). But even then, a *Seeker* must still personally "input" the *command* as *Self*. For this reason —and quite thankfully— *Solo-Processing* is possible.

TAKING FLIGHT ON THE PATHWAY

Processing Techniques are intended to treat the *Spiritual Being* or *Alpha-Spirit*; the individual themselves. It is applied by the *Alpha-Spirit*—then *Self-directed* to the "Mind-System" or even a "body" (*genetic-vehicle*), both of which are "constructs" that the *Alpha-Spirit* (*Self*, or the "I-AM" *Awareness unit*) operates, but neither of which is actually *Self*. *Fragmentation* causes *Humans* to falsely identify *Self as* the *"Mind"* or even a *"Body."*

25

The *Professional Course* lessons (booklets) are designed for the *Beginning Seeker* in mind—one that may have an understanding of theory, but with little experience in practice. That being said: each of these lessons may be used toward total *Beta-Defragmentation* within a specific area. There are also more *processes* given for each subject than may be necessary to achieve an *ultimate end-point realization* on that entire area.

Some *processes* can be treated quite lightly at first; others may require a bit of working at in order to get *"running"* well. It is important to set aside a period of time when you can be dedicated to your studies and *processing*. This period of time is referred to as a *"processing session."* The reason for this, is that when a *process* does start *running* well, it is important to be able to complete it to a satisfactory *"end-point."*

The purpose of *systematic processing* is to be able to *really* "look" at things and even determine the *considerations* we have made—or attitudes we have decided—about *Reality* as a result of those experiences. It doesn't do us much good to simply "glance"—or to *restimulate* something uncomfortable and then quickly *withdraw* from it once again, leaving more of our *attention* yet again behind and held fixedly on it.

Generally speaking, a *Seeker* continues to *run* a *process* so long as something is "happening"—which is to say, the *process* is still producing a change. Usually this is evident by the type of "answers" that a *command-line* helps a *Seeker* originate from the database of their own *Mind-System*. The *command-lines* do not "do" anything on their own. They assist a *Seeker* to direct their own attention toward increasing *Awareness*.

Of course, a *Seeker* may also cease to generate new "data" from a *process* without reaching an *"ultimate" realization* as an *"end-point."* It is possible that additional "layers" (or even other "areas") require handling before anything "deeper" is accessible. If this is the case, end the *process*. But, if a *Seeker* is *withdrawing* from something uncomfortable that was incited or stirred up, then a *process* is *run* until they feel "good" about it.

In case the thought of encountering *"turbulence"* is a concern: the techniques given as *"Opening Procedures"* of a *Formal Session* (in the *Basic Course*), and those found in the earliest lessons of the *Professional Course*, are quite useful when applied as "safety nets" for maintaining *Awareness* and *presence*, even when *Flying-Solo*.

One of the benefits to *Flying-Solo* is that *processing* is entirely *Self-determined*. This

28

already provides a certain built-in "safety" for a practitioner. Anything you *restimulate* by *Self-determinism* is *your thing*. It is not incited by external *other-determined* influences (or other "source-points" in existence) that make you an *effect*. It can be more easily handled in *processing*—or you can simply let things "cool down" and come back to it again.

While it may seem "mysterious" to beginners, a *Seeker* gets a sense for knowing how long to *run* a *process* only with practice. Once you have spent some time actually applying the *Professional Course*, there are many aspects that become "second nature" because they are, in fact, a part of our true original nature. All we have done is *"reverse engineer"* the routes of *creation* and *consideration* that are already *our own*.

LESSON FOUR:
HANDLING
HUMANITY

HANDLING THE HUMAN CONDITION

In this lesson (booklet) we will begin using the skills we previously learned for establishing a *Formal Session*—or rather, our *"presence in-session,"* which is what makes *systematic processing* possible. Here we will start to apply *processing* to specific areas that are necessary for a state of *Beta-Defragmentation*. This means handling the *Human Condition* and *confronting* our experiences in this lifetime.

For the *processing* demonstrated in earlier lessons, we mainly encouraged simply "pushing through" any *resurfacing* or *restimulated fragmentation*. It is, however, at this level of the *Professional Course* that we begin to learn how to handle *fragmentation* directly—to start actually scraping away the layers of *imprinting* and the *considerations* about *Life* and *Reality* that have been made as a result.

33

This lesson (booklet) is based on teachings previously given in the "2020 Professional Piloting Course" and contained in the text: "Metahuman Destinations (Volume II): The Universe and Mind-Body Connection."

[Note: if you have already attained any ultimate *realizations* as *end-points* for any particular area (from previous passes through this course material), then your practical instruction is to "*spot*" the moment it happened; alternatively if you have completed *Beta-Defragmentation* altogether, this material may be applied to *Alpha-Defragmentation* by *imagining/creating*, or apply the *processing* directly to the "*Backtrack*."]

COMMUNICATION AND PROTEST

Early on the *Spiritual Timeline* (or "*Backtrack*"), an *Alpha-Spirit* goes "*out-of-comm-*

unication" knowingly and selectively. This is part of how personal *Identity* is established. The *Alpha-Spirit* imposes or creates a certain "distance" for their *communication*, and "barriers" to their *perception*, so as not to experience being an integral of all *"beings"* at once.

It is in this wise that we can consider the individual's own *Spiritual Timeline* much like a *"personal identity continuum"* of an *Alpha-Spirit*—a *"ZU-Line"* that extends back to before the origins of even our "keeping track" of *time*.

As the "barriers" are originally *knowingly "Self*-imposed"—or *created* on one's own *Self-determinism*—they are usually able to be side-stepped early on the *"Backtrack"* easily with *intention*. But they are "barriers" nonetheless, and as a result, the *Alpha-Spirit* can still be "surprised" or suddenly encounter something that they weren't *aware* of, or prepared for.

Before an *Alpha-Spirit* begins to *"identify"* with *lower* material considerations for their own *Beingness* (what they truly consider *Self to Be*), they are essentially unable to be harmed—there is no "substance" for which to impact. Yet, as an early part of the formation of a basic spiritual *"identity,"* we still find the phenomenon of *"personal preference."* This might be based on *"aesthetics"* (our perception of *beauty* and *ugliness*), but it becomes an established pattern of *acceptance* and *rejection*—and increases the likelihood for blocked or misunderstood *communication*.

When undesired *communications* and *creations* are being forcefully presented to the *Alpha-Spirit*, or when their own *communications* and *creations* are rejected by others, the individual may decide to "protest" their experience of this enforcement or rejection. This is an activity modern society is quite familiar with, so we

36

will avoid using examples that are *too* specific.

However, when an individual attempts to *communicate* a *protest* and finds they are "blocked" on those *channels*, or toward a particular "audience" (*terminal*), they will increase the volume, or *create* something that is much more "physical" in nature and therefore more difficult to ignore. Something is *created*, but it is still likely to be *rejected*, and so the individual goes on continuing to *create* it "compulsively."

Often times, a "*protest fragmentation*" may be found at the heart of a "*compulsion*" — or *compulsive creation*. This is why *processing* only toward one's own *acceptance* of its existence is not enough to overcome it. The main issues must eventually be handled concerning all *flows* or *circuits* on that channel: *rejection* or *lack of acceptance* in both directions—and even the observation of others *rejecting* someone else can affect our considerations.

Communication barriers are the first factor of *fragmentation* that an *Alpha-Spirit* experiences on the *Backtrack*. Of course, because they are *Self-determined*, they are not themselves the area of *fragmentation* we target as we begin our *"defragmentation processing."* It is *"protests"* that are the first actual source of *fragmentation* that actually lowers actual ability and *Awareness* of an *Alpha-Spirit*; in this case because of the *compulsive* activity.

The instructions for basic *"protest defragmentation"* is: "spot" (*recognize*) a specific *protest*; identify what you are *creating* or *doing* to communicate that *protest*; and identify who should have received or acknowledged that communication.

A *Seeker's* "reach" on this direct method of *processing* may be limited during their first pass through the *Professional Course* material. Many of our *compulsive creations* we carry with us as *Spiritual Beings* are protesting things and aspects of existence that are not only long-forgotten, but far and beyond what is found in *this present* manifestation of a Physical Universe (*"Beta-Existence"*). As a *Seeker* increases what they *realize*, or are *aware* of, even more becomes accessible.

PROTEST DEFRAGMENTATION

As a standard *process*, the above instructions may involve communication with a *Co-Pilot*; or a *Solo-Pilot* may wish to record their answers in a *"Flight-Log."* It is best to *run* the same area of *protest* repeatedly. Focusing on *spotting* it and describing its specifics with each *run*. This allows the *process* to naturally shift to an *earlier* "protest" in memory that is in the same area or along the same *channel*. This enables you to more fully *defragment* that entire "string" or "chain."

A. *"What are you currently protesting? Describe it."*

B. *"What have you done to communicate that?"*

C. *"Who should acknowledge that communication?"*

D. *"Imagine them acknowledging your communication."*

This same basic *processing formula* (for "Circuit-1") can also be applied to handling *"protests"* on other *flows* or *circuits*. It may be preferable to rotate these other *processes* in between *processing* your own *protests*, to keep from *running* only one *flow* excessively. The following steps apply to "Circuit-2."

A. *"What about you is someone protesting?"*

B. *"What have they done to communicate that?"*

C. *"How could that be acknowledged?"*

D. *"Imagine them receiving your acknowledgment."*

And for "Circuit-3."

A. *"What are others protesting?"*

B. *"What have they done to communicate that?"*

C. *"Who should acknowledge that communication?"*

D. *"Imagine them receiving the acknowledgment."*

As *systematic processing* becomes more intricate and specific in various areas, a *processing formula*—or basic *processing command-line* ("PCL")—is given in the text that is intended to apply to a specific *"terminal"* (a person, place, thing; something with "mass"). As a *Seeker* progresses on the *Pathway*, certain areas are found to be more turbulent than others, and are therefore targeted directly.

For example: *"What have you protested about ---?"* is directly applied to any specific area (or *terminal*) that is considered a source of *turbulence* or *fragmentation* for the *Seeker*. In *Traditional Piloting* there may be a list already prepared for a *Seeker* based on earlier sessions, or else something specific that requires additional handling. If the *answer* to this PCL is "nothing," than you simply move on to the next without pressing it further.

Without having a specialized list personalized for an individual *Seeker*, we will use some general *terminals* for our *processes. These are:*

"YOUR BODY"; "YOUR FAMILY"; "JOBS"; "SOCIETY"; "HUMANS"; "LIFE ON EARTH"; "THE PHYSICAL UNIVERSE"; "SPIRITS"; and "RELIGION."

Each represents its own *process*, and are used to complete the first PCL below.

The *processing formula* is:

A. *"What have you protested about ---?"*
B. *"What did you do or create to protest that?"*

42

C. *"Who should have acknowledged it?"*

D. *"Spot an earlier similar protest and repeat."*

A *Seeker* will generally *run* this until feeling increased relief in a certain area as an *end-point*. This type of *processing* is also helpful for those *Seekers* that at first do not find accessible answers to the more direct entry-level approach of *"What are you currently protesting?"*

When a *Seeker* is comfortable with the results of a particular *process*, or when an *end-point* is reached on what is presently accessible, deeper information may usually be "scouted" by reshaping the PCL or formula as a direction to *"imagine"* something. In this case, the wording could be changed to *"What might you protest..."* or *"What would be a communication..."* &tc. The goal being always to "shine" *Awareness* on new "layers." If, however, anything seems too out-of-reach for you right

43

now, simply take it up on your additional passes through the *Professional Course.*

ACCEPTANCE AND REJECTION

A traditional way of scouting for (and handling) "protest fragmentation" attached to a particular *"terminal"* (or turbulent area), is PCL-alternation with a form of *"conceptual processing."* This generally assists a *Seeker* to free up their considerations or increase their tolerance.

A. *"What about --- might you protest?"*
B. *"What about --- could you accept?"*

Enforced inhibition—when we are prevented from *having, doing* or *being* something—often produces dramatizations of "protest." This can actually manifest in two ways. For one: there is the obvious "protest" that results from being denied something, and we still want it.

There is also another side: when this "something" is denied for too long, we may suddenly *consider* that it is "bad" and that we no longer want it. But there is still a need to connect with it on some channel, so the only solution is to "protest" *against* what we wanted but were denied, just to make sure *Self* is always right.

A. *"What have you been prevented from (having, doing, being)?"*

B. *"What protest might you have about that?"*

"Protesting" is a very specific type of *communication out-flow*. Whatever that communication may be, it is quite pointedly directed at a target recipient (involving a specific *"terminal"*). Here we see one of many instances where material from our previous lesson (booklet) on *"communication"* reoccurs on the *Pathway*.

The final *process* given for this area utilizes *Actualized Awareness* to "disintegrate" *fragmentation* directly. The theory behind its effectiveness is secondary to its application. However, let us consider that whatever we do not want around us, or in our space, is in some way being "protested against."

A. *"Get the concept of protesting the existence of ---."*

B. *"Now admire the existence of ---."*

C. *"Get the concept of you creating the existence of ---."*

This may be run repeatedly on something you are "protesting" the existence of, even if it is not concerning a dramatization of the "marching, shouting, picketing" type we are quickest to associate with the idea. We also commonly "protest" the *existence* of certain aspects regarding "school," "work," "family," and "social governance," that we experience as *reality*. But "protest" actually concerns any strong dislike or avoidance.

To be systematically effective, *protest processing* must be handled on the direct *existence* of something—and not "something about something." If you *process* a "dirt scuff" on your shoe: the protest is "the *existence* of the scuff," and not the fact that "the shoes have a scuff on them."

This systematic approach also helps us separate our *considerations* about what a thing "*Is*," as opposed to focusing on *fragmented associations* directly. The *fragmentation* here would make us more inclined to eventually not like our "*shoes*"— or even develop some other kind of automatic-response about "shoes" in general.

The "*admiration*" step may require some "build up" (with each PCL-cycle) to really acquire a good sense of. At first, a *Seeker* might simply "acknowledge" the *existence* of the thing; but with each pass of the step, try and apply an even greater sense of "*admiring*" it than previously.

Again, we are mostly concerned with freeing up a *Seeker's considerations* and *perceptive* range—undoing compulsively created *imprints* and *automated* thought. What an individual *chooses* to like or dislike as a preference is just fine so long as they are totally *Self-determined* and *Self-Honest* in their *choosing*. A *fragmented* individual only operates on a false conception of having full and total *Self-directed* control.

CHANGE AND MOTION

As a *Seeker* expects to advance upon the *Pathway,* their *willingness* to "change" must be increased. When things are difficult, there is a tendency to "clamp down" and resist change in order to avoid things getting worse. This is dramatized automatically by the *"Body"* when hurt. Essentially, the individual is trying to hold things in place—and as this starts to happen more compulsively, it becomes more difficult to change for the better.

The *Alpha-Spirit* is, itself, a *"static"* point of *Awareness* that *can* develop a distaste for "motion" (and to an extent, the *control* of *motion*). To some degree, there is a tendency to *unknowingly* hold everything "still" as a protective defense-mechanism against danger or harmful effects. Likewise, a being tends to *"keep things from going away"* as a compulsive (*unknowingly repetitive*) remedy for the experience of *loss*.

Let's shift our focus now to some *objective processing* techniques for *"Change-and-No-Change."* Each of these cycles is done five times on the same object. When you've done all three on the same object, choose a different object and do them again, five times each.

A. *"Spot the object."*

"Place your hands on it."

"Hold it absolutely still."

"Decide when to let go, and then take your hands off."

B. "Spot the object."

"Place your hands on it."

"Get a sense of keeping it from going away."

"Decide when to let go, and then take your hands off."

C. "Spot the object."

"Place your hands on it."

"Decide to move it; Decide where to move it."

"Move it to the exact spot you had decided on, and then take your hands off."

This same *systematic processing* formula may be applied to the *"Body."* For example: using your hands to grab your right leg and *"hold it absolutely still."*

Then, doing the same with the other cycles: intending to *"keep it from going away,"* and then finally *"deciding to move it"* (using your hands to lift it up and down).

Note that to *"hold it still"* and *"keep it from going away"* only appear the same at a visible level. The key difference is that, in the second one, our *intention* also includes resisting any of its efforts to move away while "holding" it there. Essentially: *our intention* is to "stop" *its effort* to "change" (or move).

This can also be practiced on other parts of the body. In some ways, it starts to establish a habit of *controlling* the *"Body"* more deliberately or *"intentionally."* Specifically in this case, an individual is *knowingly* practicing an otherwise automatic (*unknowing*) reaction to "hold" an injured or painful part of the body.

As with other *objective processing* in *Syst-*

emology, there is also a more advanced "mental" version of this exercise. It is practiced much in the same way as the physical technique, except a *Seeker* reaches "mentally" rather than with the "*Body*." In the third step: rather than "moving" the object, the PCL is to "*make it more solid*." This is done by *intention* and *sensed conceptually*.

PROCESSING "CHANGE"

In *systematic processing*, "change" is a *channel*. It is not, itself, a *terminal*; it is a *channel* between *Self* and many potential people, places, objects, *&tc*. The *communications* on this *channel* involve the three basic "circuits" described in "*Lesson 3*." The following *process* demonstrates a slightly expanded version of these *circuits*.

1. *"What would you be willing to change in another person?"*

2a. *"What would you be willing to allow someone to change in you?"*

2b. *"What would you be willing to have another person change in themselves?"*

3. *"What would you be willing to have another person change in others?"*

0. *"What would you be willing to change in yourself?"*

In the above *process*, we also introduce *"Circuit-0"* for the first time in the *Professional Course*. It is not so much a communicative *flow* to others, but from *Self* to *Self*. In this case, *Self* is always the *"terminal."* In *Systemology*, this is sometimes referred to as a *"beingness postulate"* (or *"Alpha-Thought"*) when *Self directs* a decision that something *"Is"* —or about how something will either *"Be"* or *"Not-Be."*

In the end, all areas of *processing* are ultimately handling one's own *"postulates."*

In essence, it is *"Alpha-Thought"* that we are working up to reaching and mastering with the *Pathway.* If we were truly able to "change our mind" completely from within the *Human Condition,* we wouldn't remain in this state; so there are obviously some barriers of *fragmentation* that need to be cleared for this to be possible again.

To continue demonstrating how to *process* the area of "change," we will utilize the *"Analytical Recall"* technique introduced in *"Lesson 2."* Each circuit is treated in its own *process* containing two PCL. The PCL are alternated repeatedly until a *Seeker* cannot readily access more answers. Then go to the next *process* and do the same. After all four are completely *run,* cycle them again and see if any new answers are produced.

1a. *"Recall changing something."*
1b. *"Recall stopping something from changing."*

2a. *"Recall someone changing something."*

2b. *"Recall someone stopping something from changing."*

3a. *"Recall society changing."*

3b. *"Recall society resisting change."*

0a. *"Recall changing yourself."*

0b. *"Recall stopping yourself from changing."*

And now let's treat this more *"conceptually"* following the same basic instruction from the previous four *processes*. Notice we are using the words *"could"* and *"would"* to expand our range of free *consideration*.

1a. *"What could you change?"*

1b. *"What would you leave unchanged?"*

2a. *"What could change you?"*

2b. *"What would leave you unchanged?"*

3a. *"What could change others?"*

3b. *"What would leave others unchanged?"*

0a. *"What could you change about yourself?"*

0b. *"What would you leave unchanged about yourself?"*

For additional *objective processing* in this area:

"(Look around the room.) Spot something you would be willing (and able) to change; then change it."

"Spot something you find acceptable to remain the same; then leave it unchanged."

And finally:

A. *"What must be changed?"*

B. *"What must not be changed?"*

C. *"What is acceptable to leave uncontrolled?"*

D. *"What can you control comfortably?"*

As an entry-point to directly handling the *Human Condition*, we have emphasized the areas of "protest" and "change." Total *defragmentation* in these areas will likely take a second pass through the *Professional Course*, and possibly several cycles through the *processing* in this one lesson (booklet) alone.

The ultimate *end-point* we are reaching for in this area would include the elimination of any compulsive tendencies in the areas of "protest" and "change." For example: a freedom from the *need* to change people, or prevent them from changing, in order to find them more acceptable. And, on the other side: an increased willingness to *allow* change in one's environment, or among others, without feeling a *need* to become involved.

HUMAN PROBLEMS

The type of *"problems"* handled with *Systematic Processing* are those things that tend to "hang up" in our lives—or else continuously exist without a perceivable solution. This is quite different from the kind of "logic problems" you might think of in relation to, for example, *"mathematics."*

Human Problems remain suspended in space and time as *fragmentation* because personal *attention-energy* remains compulsively fixed on them as a "problem." We are speaking of logical *"conflicts"*—or where two "things" (or *"considerations"*) remain fixedly in *opposition* to one another indefinitely.

For example: the *"problem"* of *how* to add additional rooms to your property is easily solved by logic. This would require a knowledge and means for construction, or hiring a contractor. This is not a *real* "problem." *Real problems* would require these two things to be *oppositional*—and they obviously are not.

But could this somehow become a *real problem?* Yes. If an individual *considers* that they both *"need an additional room"* and *"have no financial means to pay for it,"* then it could develop into a *"problem"* that suspends or fixes the individual's *attention-energy* compulsively.

These two things—*"needing rooms"* and *"no money for it"* are obviously in *opposition*. The conditions cannot exist simultaneously and ever provide any kind of "solution." When not properly handled, this kind of *problem* has a tendency to suspend *attention-energy* indefinitely, which is the nature of the *fragmentation*.

Ideally, an individual will *realize* that one side or other of the *problem* has to be figured out. It is not a balanced equation to be solved as itself. Yet, the longer it remains suspended as a *problem*, the greater of an *energetic-mass* it becomes as *fragmentation*. More and more *attention* is fed into it as purely a *problem*.

In this example, the only "solution" would be to treat either the "*need for more rooms*" or the "*lack of funds.*" Both of these are *considerations* only. The fact that they collide during one's lifetime into a *mass* is simply unfortunate. Either an individual would have to find an *alternative* to the "*need for more rooms*" (such as better utilizing existing space), or they would find a way to "*make more money*" or build "*more economically.*"

One of the reasons *Human Problems* unfold this way is because of how much *attention-energy* they demand once they are treated as a *mass*. They have a tendency to "pull down" an individual's *Actualized Awareness* in a way that keeps them from *considering* one "side" or the other, because they only "see" the *mass*.

When the *mass* becomes a turbulent source of *fragmentation*, it may have "grown" to a state that causes the individual to feel overwhelmed (*confused*) and unwilling to *confront* it.

For example: every time the individual starts to think about "*more room,*" the turbulence associated with "*money problems*" is triggered or *restimulated*, and hence they cannot think clearly about it. Then, whenever they start to try to *confront* the issue of "*money,*" the worries about "*space*" become a sudden distraction.

As you can see: this individual's *problems* will cyclically continue and persist in this wise unless there is some resolution or intervention from an outside source. Unless the *fragmentation* is solved, however, even good fortune and charity from others will not keep the individual from falling prey to this pattern again. Their thoughts and behavior will *unknowingly* still find there way into treating this *problem* as *reality*.

Our observation of this in others also inhibits our natural desire to *"help"* others. We've seen many times that our intervention to "solve" someone's *problems* directly will not always work out. They end up in the same mess again, or it somehow seems to "backfire" on *us*. This can cause us to develop *fragmentation* in the area of *"help"* which is quite detrimental to advancement on the *Pathway*.

Therefore, in total, the main areas for *systematic processing* that we focus on in this lesson, concerning *Humanity* and *Human Problems*, are: PROTEST, CHANGE, PROBLEMS and HELP.

DEFRAGMENTING PROBLEMS

The basic *processing* of *problems* begins with the PCL: *"What is the problem?"* This causes the *mass* to *resurface* directly. Then, a *Seeker* can *run* multiple cycles of: *"spot the problem"* and *"spot something about the problem"* and then *"spot the problem"* again. This allows a *Seeker* to start to control their *attention* in seeing the *"mass"* and then seeing a *"point"* of the *mass* rather than the whole. This may change how one *perceives* the *mass* thereafter.

When we say *"see,"* what we really mean is *"confront"*—and more specifically, *confront "As-It-Is."* This is something a continuing *Seeker/student* from previous lessons will be familiar with. Not only do we *process* toward *confronting* what the *Seeker* is presently perceiving as a *problem*, but in doing so, it is likely that other related or similar underlying *problems* will also *resurface* to *confront*—and this is how *defragmentation* ensues.

The standard *processing* method of the above technique is:

"What is the problem?"

"What part of that problem could you confront?"

Once a *Seeker* is able to "spot" both *opposing* "sides" of the *problem*, the most effective application for these types of techniques would involve alternately "*spotting*" (or "*confronting*") something on *each* "side" of the *problem* as the *process* is repeatedly *run*.

An *Alpha-Spirit* is an "*eternal being*" that likes to be interested in things. *Eternity* is a long time—certainly long enough for us to have our fondness of "*games*" and "*solving problems*" get turned against us. In the case of the *Human Condition*, any lingering compulsive interests in *creating universes* and *games*, to add richness and variety to *Existence*, is reduced to *creating problems* for ourselves. By this we are always ensured to have "something" to *do*. A *fragmented* being will always prefer a "*fragmented somethingness*" over "*Nothingness*."

In these next *processes*, we are not trying to "solve" a *problem*. A *Seeker* "spots" the

64

problem and then follows the next PCL, which starts with *"imagine."* By *"imagine,"* we mean to create, invent, or visualize something. This should be an original *creation* and not an automatically (*reactively*) *recalled* event or mental image, *&tc.*

By doing this *knowingly*, the *fragmentation* that causes the *"compulsive creation"* of *problems* comes into view, or at the very least "loosens" or "softens" for later additional *processing*.

The following three *processes* are *run* individually. If after *running* the first multiple times, the *problem* either seems more solid or the turbulence has not lessened, go to the next, and so on. They are all essentially working to accomplish the same thing and can be repeated as many times as is necessary.

"Spot the problem."
"Imagine a problem of similar magnitude."

"Spot the problem."

"Imagine something that is worse than that problem."

"Spot the problem."

"Imagine a game that would be more interesting than that problem."

A *real problem* is only brought to a *resolution* by handling it or *confronting* it *"As-It-Is."* Otherwise, whatever *fragmented* "solution" is applied to it will simply bury the original *problem* deeper and also create a new one. For example: *"borrowing money"* for the *"additional room"* only adds to the chain of complications attached to the original *"not enough money"* side of the *problem*. The individual still doesn't have enough and still has to pay for it, but now, presumably with interest. It only *avoids* the original "face" of the unsolvable *problem*.

We can apply some *processing* to this area by treating the stores of information coll-

lected (communicated) on the "circuits."
A continuing *Seeker* will, by now, be familiar with how to *run* this type of PCL-series:

1. *"Spot the problem."*

   "What solutions have you had for that problem?"

2. *"What problem has someone had with you?"*

   "What solutions have they had for that problem?"

3. *"What problem has someone had with others?"*

   "What solutions have they had for that problem?"

The total handling of *"a problem"* in *processing* is not the same as an *end-point realization* on the total area of *"problems"* in general; but it is a goal. Again, this is not something we are pushing a *Seeker* to expect on the first-pass of this course.

However, the *"ultimate process"* for this area is:

"Spot the problem."

"What part of that problem could you be responsible for?"

This is *run* until a *Seeker* no longer produces new answers (or until the *end-realization* for the *problem* or problems). Then *run*:

"Spot the problem."

"What part of that problem could you admit to causing?"

The ultimate *end-realization* on a single *problem* and the entire area of *problems* is: an individual is responsible for creating their own perceived problems. *Systematic Processing* is not intended as a "therapy" to *"solve problems"* but instead, a means of solving the need to handle or consider things *as real problems*.

ON THE SUBJECT OF HELP

"Help" is high-level *communication*. To be *"helped"* —to be *willing* to give and receive *help*—requires being *in communication*. Of course, we know that *help* is frequently taken advantage of, or even used as a control mechanism to enforce a *reality* on another. But to be *Self-actualized*, no *fragmentation* can inhibit our *willingness* to *help* and be *helped*.

Help is a difficult area for many individuals due to long *imprint*-"chains" comprised of many unfortunate experiences. Even when *help* is genuine—with "no strings attached"—it sometimes fails. When this cannot be *confronted* directly, the "weight" of accumulated failures builds up *mass* as *"help fragmentation."*

As a high-power *flow* of *communication*, *"help"* also has the unique ability for breaking down or surpassing what would otherwise be a *"communication barrier."* For example: if one could find ways in which to *help* an enemy and for an enemy to *help* them, the conceptual "walls" forged with hatred and war could dissolve.

For *Solo-Processing*, it is better to emphasize the "positive" side of an area in *processing*—or at the very least, being sure to alternate *spotting* the "positive" side along with the "negatives." Doing so assists a *Solo-Pilot* to push through the *fragmented-masses* that may have developed along these channels without too easily being overwhelmed by *turbulence* or distraction.

HELP DEFRAGMENTATION

In first approaching *Help-Defragmentation*, it may be best for a *Seeker* (as *Solo-Pilot*) to direct their PCL toward general "*terminal*" areas, rather than specific examples or individuals. This expands the range of *considerations* directly within the *process* (or during the *session*). It also promotes *defragmentation* on the greater "chains" that extend farther on the "*Backtrack*" (or personal "*Spiritual Timeline*").

Systematic Processing is really meant to improve how a *Seeker* handles an area in general. The seemingly current or presently restimulated "*problems*" and "*upsets*" that are more specifically targeted in some *processes* is merely a factor of *running* those areas. If something is presently triggering activity in a certain area, that would obviously require handling before one can get total stable control over that entire area.

Much like some of the other general areas of *subjective processing* already explored in the *Professional Course* series, we will use PCL that employ the words "*could*" in order to free up our *considerations* further *in-session*. This means that there is no pressure, directive, or insistence, that a *Seeker* actually "act" on any of these *considerations*. The "*answers*" do not all necessarily even have to be logical or realistic. We are simply treating all aspects of the entire area *systematically* in our *processing*.

These "*help-processes*" are the final *defragmentation* techniques provided in this lesson. They are simple *repetitive processes* using alternating PCL. A *Seeker* repetitively *runs* the PCL, simply *spotting* (*locating, identifying, recognizing in Awareness, &tc.*) the various ways you *could help* or *would be willing to help*, &tc.

When cycling though these *processes*, a *Seeker* is often pushing through "mental barriers" of *consideration* and other *postulates* (or "*Alpha-Thought*") generated from a state of *fragmentation*. "*Answers*" may not always be immediately obvious, but they tend to *surface* in "layers." This applies to more than just *Help-processing.*

So, a *Seeker* may sometimes reach a point in the *process* where they really have to reach to come up with something and still its a struggle or they can't "find" an "*answer*" in their data-banks; but then something new "occurs" to them, and they suddenly start rapidly *out-flowing* a whole new group of "*answers.*" This type of "*flash*" or "*sudden realization*" is a large part of what we are after when using these *processes.*

When listing your "*answers*" in *Solo-processing*, it is quite acceptable to simply "*read/run*" the PCL *once*, then write down as many answers that come to mind; or if you only come up with one or two and feel your mind kind of "wandering" afterward, then you might "*read/run*" again to reorient yourself. When you feel you have completed one *process*, simply go to the next.

Willingness to Help

1. *"Who or what would you be willing to help?"*

2. *"Who or what would you be willing to have help you?"*

3. *"Who or what would you be willing to have others help?"*

General Help Process

1. *"How could you help someone else?"*

2a. *"How could someone else help you?"*

2b. *"How could someone else help themselves?"*

3. *"How could someone else help others?"*

0. *"How could you help yourself?"*

Past Help (*four separate processes*)

1. *"What help have you given to someone?"*

   "What help have you not given to someone?"

2. *"What help has someone given to you?"*

   "What help has someone not given to you?"

3. *"What help have others given to others?"*

   "What help have others not given to others?"

0. *"What help have you given yourself?"*

   "What help have you not given yourself?"

To demonstrate more specific *Help-processing* in this lesson, it is necessary that we again employ a *processing formula*.

Here, a *Seeker* uses the basic structure for separate *processes*, each of which may target a specific *terminal*.

Suggested terminals (in chronological order) for use are: "BODY," "CHILD," "PARENT," "LOVER," "TEACHER," "OFFICER," "PRIEST," "POLITICIAN," "ANIMAL," "TREE," "SPIRIT," and "GOD."

The *processing formula* is:

A. *"How could you help a ---?"*

B. *"How could a --- help you?"*

C. *"How could a --- help another?"*

D. *"How could another help a ---?"*

E. *"How could a --- help themselves?"*

What generally occurs when *processing* an area intensely—such as demonstrated with the above *Help-processes*—is that the individual's own personal *"definition"* for (or *consideration* of) a specific area—such as *Help*—changes many times. It is from the viewpoint or point-of-view (POV) of that new *"definition"* that the next layer of *"answers"* originates from. This is how a *Seeker* *"systematically"* frees their true power of choice.

Much of what is given as *Help-processing* really serves to assist in breaking down those "barriers" and *masses* that are *created* by the *Seeker*—even if *unknowingly*—which blocks their *Awareness* from truly contacting, experiencing, and therefore, *confronting*, this physical existence. It is only once these *"gates"* begin to be opened—once these *"walls"* we've *created* begin to break down—that we will *realize* we have only been sealing up our own entrapment this entire time.

- - - -

Working through this fourth lesson (booklet) of the *Professional Course,* in combination with the previous three (and the *Basic Course*), marks completion of "*Systemology Level-1.*" It demonstrates the first required step, an increase of *Actualized Awareness,* necessary to *actually* "improve"—which is to say, a *willingness* to "change" for the better—as the *Seeker* progresses further on the *Pathway-to-Ascension.*

The Systemology Professional Course
continues in the next lesson booklet:
FREE YOUR SPIRIT

GLOSSARY

actualization : to make actual, not just potential; to bring into full solid Reality; to realize fully in *Awareness* as a "thing."

agreement (reality) : unanimity of opinion of what is "thought" to be known; an accepted arrangement of how things are; things we consider as "real" or as an "is" of "reality"; a consensus of what is real as made by standard-issue (common) participants; what an individual contributes to or accepts as "real"; in *Systemology*, a synonym for *"reality."*

alpha : the first, primary, basic, superior or beginning of some form; in *Systemology*, referring to the state of existence operating on spiritual archetypes and postulates, will and intention "exterior" to the low-level condensation and solidarity of energy and matter as the 'physical universe' (*beta*).

alpha-spirit : a "spiritual" *Life*-form; the "true" *Self* or I-AM; the *individual*; the spiritual (*alpha*) *Self* that is animating the (*beta*) physical body or "*genetic vehicle*" using a continuous *Lifeline* of spiritual ("*ZU*") energy; an individual spiritual (*alpha*) entity possessing no physical mass or measurable waveform (motion) in the Physical Universe as itself, so it animates the (*beta*) physical body or "*genetic vehicle*" as a catalyst to experience *Self*-determined causality in effect within the *Physical Universe*; a singular unit or point of *Spiritual Awareness* that is *Aware* that it is *Aware*.

alpha thought : the highest spiritual *Self-determination* over creation and existence exercised by an Alpha-Spirit; the Alpha range of pure *Creative Ability* based on direct postulates and considerations of *Beingness*; spiritual qualities comparable to "thought" but originating in Alpha-existence, independently superior to a Mind-System.

ascension : actualized *Awareness* elevated to the point of true "spiritual existence" exterior to *beta existence*. An "Ascended Master" is one who has returned to an incarnation on Earth as an inherently *Enlightened One*, demonstrable in their words and actions; they have the ability to *Self-direct* the "Mind" and "Body" as *Self* (as a "Spirit"); and to maintain consciousness as a personal identity continuum with the same *Self-directed* control and communication of Will-Intention that is exercised, actualized and developed deliberately during one's present incarnation.

associative knowledge : significance or meaning of a facet or aspect assigned to (or considered to have) a direct relationship with another facet; to connect or relate ideas or facets of existence with one another; in traditional systems logic, an equivalency of significance or meaning between facets or sets that are grouped together, such as in $(a + b) + c = a + (b + c)$; in Systemology, erroneous associative knowledge is assignment of the same value to all facets or parts considered as related (even when they are not actually so), such as in $a = a,\ b = a,\ c = a$ and so forth without distinction.

attention : active use of *Awareness* toward a specific aspect or thing; the act of "attending" with the presence of *Self*; a direction of focus or concentration of *Awareness* along a particular channel or conduit or toward a particular terminal node or communication termination point; the Self-directed concentration of personal energy as a combination of observation, thought-waves and consideration; focused application of *Self-Directed Awareness*.

awareness : the highest sense of-and-as *Self* in knowing and being as I-AM (the *Alpha-Spirit*); the extent of beingness directed as a viewpoint (POV) experienced by *Self* as knowingness.

beta (existence) : all manifestation in the "Physical Universe" (KI, in *Zuism*); the conditions of *Awareness* for the *Alpha-spirit* (*Self*) as a physical organic *Lifeform* or "*genetic vehicle*" in which it experiences causality in the *Physical Universe*.

charge : to fill or furnish with a quality; to supply with energy; to lay a command upon; in *Systemology*—to imbue with intention; to overspread with emotion; personal energy stores and significances entwined as fragmentation in mental images, reactive-response encoding and intellectual (and/or) programmed beliefs.

circuit : a circular path or loop; a closed-path within a system that allows a flow; a pattern or action or wave movement that follows a specific route or potential path only; in *Systemology*, "*communication processing*" pertaining to a specific *flow* of energy or information along a particular channel.

communication : successful transmission of information, data, energy (&tc.) along a message line, with a reception of feedback; an energetic flow of intention to cause an effect (or duplication) at a distance; the personal energy moved or acted upon by will or else 'selective directed attention'; the 'messenger action' used to transmit and receive energy across a medium; also relay of energy, a message or signal—or even locating a personal POV (viewpoint) for the Self—along the *ZU-line*.

compulsion : a failure to be responsible for the dynamics of control—starting, stopping or altering—on a particular channel and/or regarding a particular terminal in existence; an energetic flow with the appearance of being 'stuck' on the action it is already doing or by the control of some automatic mechanism.

confront : to come around in front of; to be in the presence of; to stand in front of, or in the face of; to meet "face-to-face" or "face-up-to"; additionally, in *Systemology*, to fully tolerate or acceptably withstand an encounter with a particular manifestation or encounter.

consideration : careful analytical reflection of all aspects; deliberation; determining the significance of a "thing" in relation to similarity or dissimilarity to other "things"; evaluation of facts and importance of certain facts; thorough examination of all aspects related to, or important for, making a decision; the analysis of consequences and estimation of significance when making decisions; in *Systemology*, the postulate or Alpha-Thought that defines the state of beingness for what something "*is*."

continuum : a continuous enduring uninterrupted sequence or condition; all gradients on a *spectrum*; measuring quantitative variation with gradual transition on a spectrum without demonstrating discontinuity or separate parts.

control : the ability to start, change or start some action or flow of energy; the capacity to originate, change or stop some mode of human behavior by some implication, physical or psychological means to ensure compliance (voluntarily or involuntarily); communication relayed from an operative center or organizational cluster, which incites new activity elsewhere in a system (or along the *ZU-line*).

defragmentation : the *reparation* of wholeness; collecting all dispersed parts to reform an original whole; a process of removing "*fragmentation*" in data or knowledge to provide a clear understanding; applying techniques and processes that promote a *holistic* interconnected *alpha* state, favoring observational *Awareness* of continuity in all spiritual and physical systems; in *Systemology*, a "*Seeker*" achieving actualized "*Self-Honest Awareness*" is said to be in a basic state of *beta-defragmentation*, whereas *Alpha-defragmentation* is the rehabilitation of the *creative ability*, managing the *Spiritual Timeline* and the POV of *Self* as Alpha-Spirit (I-AM).

fragmentation : breaking into parts and scattering the pieces; the *fractioning* of wholeness or the *fracture* of a holistic interconnected *alpha* state, favoring observational *Awareness* of perceived connectivity between parts; *discontinuity*; separation of a totality into parts; in *Systemology*, a person outside of *Self-Honesty* is said to be operating from a *fragmented* state.

flow : movement across (or through) a channel (or conduit); a direction of active energetic motion, typically distinguished as either an *in-flow*, *out-flow* or *cross-flow*.

genetic-vehicle : a physical *Life*-form; the physical (*beta*) body that is animated/controlled by the (*Alpha*) *Spirit* using a continuous *Spiritual Lifeline* (ZU); a physical (*beta*) organic receptacle and catalyst for the (*Alpha*) *Self* to operate "causes" and experience "effects" within the *Physical Universe*.

holistic : the examination of interconnected systems as encompassing something greater than the *sum* of their "parts."

Human Condition : a standard default state of Human experience that is generally accepted to be the extent of its potential identity (*beingness*) —currently treated as *Homo Sapiens Sapiens,* but which is scheduled for replacement by *Homo Novus* (the "New Human").

identification : the association of *identity* to a thing; a label or fixed data-set associated to what a thing is; association "equals" a thing, the "equals" being key; an equality of all things in a group, for example, an "apple" identified with all other "apples"; the reduction of "I-AM"-*Self* from a *Spiritual Beingness* to an "identity" of some form.

identity : the collection of energy and matter—including memory—across a "*Spiritual Timeline*" that we consider as "I" of *Self*, but the "I" is an individual and not an identification with anything other than *Self* as *Alpha-Spirit*.

identity-system : the application of the *ZU-line* as "I"—the continuous expression of *Self* as *Awareness* across a "*Spiritual Timeline.*"

imprint : to strongly impress, stamp, mark (or outline) onto a softer 'impressible' substance; to mark with pressure onto a surface; in *Systemology*, used to indicate permanent Reality impressions marked by frequencies, energies or interactions experienced during periods of emotional distress, pain, unconsciousness, loss, enforcement, or something antagonistic to physical (personal) survival, all of which are are stored with other reactive response-mechanisms at lower-levels of *Awareness* as opposed to the active memory database and proactive processing center of the Mind; an experiential "memory-set" that may later resurface—be triggered or stimulated artificially—as Reality, of which similar responses will be engaged automatically; holographic-like imagery "stamped" onto consciousness as composed of energetic *facets* tied to the "snap-shot" of an experience.

pilot : a professional steersman responsible for healthy functional operation of a ship toward a specific destination; in *Systemology*, an intensive trained individual qualified to specially apply *Systemology Processing* to assist other *Seekers* on the *Pathway*.

presence : a quality of some thing (*energy/matter*) being "present" in space-time; personal orientation of *Self* as an *Awareness* (*POV*) located in present space-time (environment) and communicating with extant energy-matter.

processing command line (PCL) or **command line** : a directed input; a specific command using highly selective language for *Systemology Processing*; a predetermined directive statement (cause) intended to focus concentrated attention (effect).

processing, systematic : the inner-workings or "through-put" result of systems; in *Systemology*, a method of applied spiritual technology used toward personal Self-Actualization; methods of selective directed attention, communicated language and associative imagery that increases personal control of the human condition.

protest : a response-communication objecting an enforcement (or a rejection of a prior communication); an effort to cancel, rewrite or destroy the existence of a previous creation or communication; unwillingness to be the *Point-of-View* of effect or (receipt-point) for a communication.

realization : the clear perception of an understanding; a consideration or understanding on what is "actual"; to make "real" or give "reality" to so as to grant a property of "beingness" or "being as it is"; the state or instance of coming to an *Awareness*; in *Systemology*, "gnosis" or true knowledge achieved during *systematic processing*; achievement of a new (or "higher") cognition, true knowledge or perception of Self; a consideration of reality or assignment of meaning.

responsibility : the *ability* to *respond*; the extent of mobilizing *power* and *understanding* an individual maintains as *Awareness* to enact *change*; the proactive ability to *Self-direct* and make decisions independent of an outside authority.

Seeker : an individual on the *Pathway to Self-Honesty*; a practitioner of *Mardukite Systemology* or *Systemology Processing*, that is working toward *Spiritual Ascension*.

Self-actualization : bringing the full potential of the Human spirit into Reality; expressing full capabilities and creativeness of the *Alpha-Spirit*.

Self-determinism : the freedom to act, clear of external control or influence; the personal control of Will to direct intention.

Self-honesty : the basic or original *alpha* state of *being* and *knowing*; clear and present total *Awareness* of-and-as *Self*, in its most basic and true proactive expression of itself as *Spirit* or *I-AM*—free of artificial attachments, perceptive filters and other emotionally-reactive or mentally-conditioned programming imposed on the human condition by the systematized physical world; the ability to experience existence without judgment.

spiritual timeline : a continuous stream of moment-to-moment *Mental Images* (or a record of experiences) that defines the "past" of a spiritual being (or *Alpha-Spirit*) and which includes impressions (*imprints, &tc.*) from all life-incarnations and significant spiritual events the being has encountered; in Systemology, also "*backtrack.*"

Systemology : a modern tradition of applied religious philosophy and spiritual technology based on *Arcane Tablets* (in combination with "*general systemology*" and "*games theory*") developed in the New Age underground by Joshua Free in 2011 as an advanced futurist extension of the *Mardukite Research Org.*; also known as "*Mardukite Systemology,*" "*Metahuman Systemology*" and "*Spiritual Systemology.*"

terminal (node) : a point, end, or mass, on a line; a connection point for closing an electric circuit, such as a post on a battery terminating at each end of its own systematic function; a point of connectivity with other points; in systems, a contact point of interaction; a point of interaction with other points.

turbulence : a quality or state of distortion or disturbance that creates irregularity of a flow or pattern; the quality or state of aberration on a line (such as ragged edges) or the emotional "turbulent feelings" attached to a particular flow or terminal node; a violent, haphazard or disharmonious commotion (such as in the ebb of gusts and lulls of wind action).

willingness : the state of conscious Self-determined ability and interest (directed attention) to *Be*, *Do* or *Have*; a Self-determined consideration to reach, face up to (*confront*) or manage some "mass" or energy; the extent to which an individual considers themselves able to participate, act or communicate along some line, to put attention or intention on the line, or to produce (create) an effect.

ZU : the ancient Sumerian cuneiform sign for the archaic verb—"*to know*," "*knowingness*" or "*awareness*"; in *Mardukite Zuism and Systemology*, the active energy/matter of the "Spiritual Universe" (AN) experienced as a *Lifeforce* or *consciousness* that imbues living forms extant in the "Physical Universe" (KI); "*Spiritual Life Energy*"; energy demonstrated by the WILL of an actualized *Alpha-Spirit* in the "Spiritual Universe" (AN), which impinges its *Awareness* into the Physical Universe (KI), animating/controlling *Life* for its experience of *beta-existence* along an individual Alpha-Spirit's personal *Identity-continuum*, called a *ZU-line*.

Zu-Line : a theoretical construct in *Mardukite Zuism and Systemology* demonstrating *Spiritual Life Energy* (ZU) as a personal individual "continuum" of Awareness interacting with all Spheres of Existence on the Standard Model of Systemology; a spectrum of potential variations and interactions of a monistic continuum or singular *Spiritual Life Energy (ZU)* demonstrated on the Standard Model; an energetic channel of potential POV and "locations" of Beingness, demonstrated in early Systemology materials as an individual Alpha-Spirit's personal *Identity-continuum*, potentially connecting *Awareness (ZU)* of *Self* with *"Infinity"* simultaneous with all points considered in existence; a symbolic demonstration of the *"Life-line"* on which *Awareness (ZU)* extends from the direction of the "Spiritual Universe" (AN) in its true original *alpha state* through an entire possible range of activity resulting in its *beta state* and control of a *genetic-entity* occupying the *Physical Universe (KI)*.

Fundamentals of Systemology
in six
Basic Course Lesson Booklets

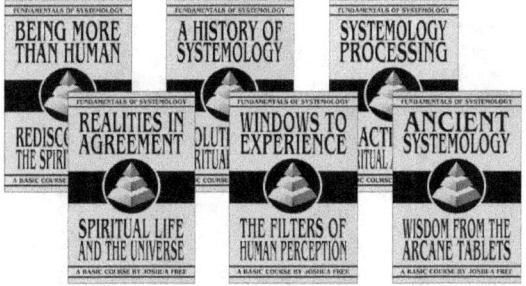

Also
available
as a
six-in-one
hardcover
edition!

THE SYSTEMOL

Seekers and students of the *Basic Course* and *Professional Course* will also be interested in the *Advanced Series* of the *Systemology Core*. These volumes are a complete chronological record of the Mardukite New Thought developments from the Systemology Society, published in 2019 through 2023.

The *Systemology Core* begins with the first professional publication released when the *Mardukite Systemology Society* emerged from the underground in 2019, with: *"The Tablets of Destiny Revelation."*

OGY PATHWAY

PUBLISHED BY THE **JOSHUA FREE** IMPRINT REPRESENTING

The Mardukite Academy of Systemology

mardukite.com

www.ingramcontent.com/pod-product-compliance
Lightning Source LLC
Chambersburg PA
CBHW071211120626
46546CB00006B/2511